YORKSHIRE DIALECT

compiled by Arnold Kellett

Dalesman

First published in Great Britain 2008 by Dalesman
The Gatehouse, Skipton Castle,
Skipton, North Yorkshire BD23 1AL

Reprinted 2009, 2011, 2013, 2014, 2016, 2017, 2018, 2019

Text © Arnold Kellett 2008
Illustrations © Peter Kearney 2008

ISBN 978-1-85568-257-3

Printed in China for Latitude Press Ltd.

Introduction

Real Yorkshire dialect is rapidly becoming a thing of the past. Today we mostly hear what members of the Yorkshire Dialect Society think of as 'local speech'. This has the traditional accent and intonation, but hardly any of the special words and idiomatic phrases which once made Yorkshire speech so distinctive.

It is easy to see why dialect is disappearing: rapid social change, with the old dialect terms becoming obsolete along with the objects they once described, both in town and country; to say nothing of the constant pressure of education and the media to conform.

Even so, though speakers of real dialect are an endangered species, we at least have the opportunity to set down and record some of that lively and colourful speech which is still remembered with affection.

This is what I have tried to do in my various dialect books, a flavour of which I now offer for your interest and amusement in this 'Little Book' – based on the wonderful experience of growing up in Wibsey in the West Riding, and then long contact with dialect speakers in various parts of the old North and East Ridings.

Dr Arnold Kellett

Acknowledgements

Thanks are gratefully made for the use of small quotations from the sources noted in the text.

'He spoke the King's English in one circle – and King's Yorkshire in another.'

(Robert Southey, 'The Doctor')

The earliest roots of Yorkshire speech are in the Celtic language of the Ancient Britons (around 500 BC). For example:

pen head (eg Pen Hill, Wensleydale)

chevin ridge (eg Otley Chevin)

isura swift (eg River Ure)

brock badger

coble East Coast fishing boat

brat apron, smock
(eg a woolsorter's brat)

A Celtic style of counting sheep was once used by dialect-speaking Dales shepherds. In Wensleydale, for example, it began:

*1. Yan, 2. Tean, 3. Tither, 4. Mither,
5. Pip, 6. Teaser, 7. Leaser, 8. Catra,
9. Horna, 10. Dick, 11. Yan-dick,
12. Tean-dick ... 15. Bumper,
16. Yan-a-bum ... 20. Jigger.*

The Germanic speech of the Angles (from the fifth century) gave Yorkshire dialect sounds with characteristically short vowels. For example:

finnd, blinnd, nivver, onny, ovver / ower, oppen, telled, lang, watter, fatther, frozzen, spokken, wokken.

Typical short dialect words derived
from the speech of the Angles are,
for example:

nobbut only, *oft* often, *summat* something,
owt anything, *nowt* nothing
(both the latter usually pronounced with
the vowel, not like Standard English
'now', but more like 'aw-oo')

Because dialect uses words from the Old English of the Angles, sometimes it might sound as though there is an ignorant misuse of a word like *starve*, for example. From the old verb 'steorfan' (to suffer intensely) this can mean to suffer from the cold, as well as from hunger, as in the examples:

Ah wor fair starved aht theeare
I was really cold out there

Ee! Tha's a reight starved-un!
(Said to a person who easily feels cold)

A nice dialect verb, lost from Standard English, is *thoil*, from Old English 'tholian' (to bear, endure). So when a Yorkshire person says '*Nay, Ah can't thoil t' brass*', this doesn't mean 'I can't afford it', but 'I can't bring myself to spend my money on this particular item'.

Yorkshire dialect has two main divisions – that of the West Riding, derived from speech in the old kingdom of Mercia, and that of the North and East Ridings (very similar to each other) derived from speech in the old kingdom of Northumbria (i.e. the land north of the Humber). West Riding dialect covers roughly the area south of the River Wharfe.

The three Ridings ER, WR and NR

Examples of dialect differences –
West Riding (left) and North and
East Ridings:

down	*dahn*	*doon*
none	*nooan*	*neean*
coat	*coit*	*cooat*
home	*'oame*	*yam*
eyes	*een*	*ees*
sweets	*spice*	*goodies*
I am	*Ah'm*	*Ah's*

13

In the ninth century the Vikings
added their own words to our dialect.
Apart from topographical terms like
beck, *fell* and *-gate* (eg Kirkgate, the
way to the church) there are many
common words such as
laik to play, *addle* to earn, *lig* to lie,
stee ladder, *kist* wooden chest, *lug* ear,
neave fist, *lop* flea.

Common dialect phrases derived from the speech of the Vikings:

Ah'm bahn I'm going

Gerr aht o' mi gate! Get out of my way!

Ey up! Look out! (Also an expression of surprise, etc)

The Normans, from 1066, tried to impose the French language on us, and about a third of English is derived from it. Norman terms surviving only in dialect include:

urchin

arran spider

urchin hedgehog

buffit low stool (dialect preserves the
original Norman meaning, modern
French *buffet* meaning 'sideboard')

fent remnant of cloth

frumenty wheaten porridge

cham'er upper room, bedroom

Yorkshire dialect has some odd past participles, including the following:

brokken broken, *brussen* burst,
chozzen chosen, *etten* eaten,
fergetten forgotten, *fun* found, *getten* got,
gi'en given, *putten* put, *rivven* torn,
shakked shaken, *ta'en*, taken,
tenged stung, *tret* treated, *wed* married.

A good example of how children used to cling to their dialect, even when corrected by teachers, is the use of an old past participle by the lad who replied, when his teacher asked him what was wrong with what he'd written:

'Nay, miss! Ah've gooan an' putten 'putten', when Ah owt to 'a' putten 'put'!'

tha in the West Riding and *thoo* in the North and East Ridings must be used with caution. The familiar form of 'you' and 'your' (*thee/tha/ta, thoo, thy, thine*) is only for relations and those who are accepted as friends. Over-familiar folk are told (in the West Riding):

Ey! Dooan't thee thee-tha me! Tha thee-tha's them 'at thee-tha's thee!

Yorkshire folk, especially those in charge of others, have little time for stupidity and incompetence, as is shown by various pronouncements on character. For example:

as daft as a brush

as simple as a suckin' duck

as sackless as a booat-'oss

as gaumless as a gooise nicked i' t' 'eead

What's the weather like? For rainy days we could say:

It's black ovver Bill's mother's
It's ossin ter slaht coming on to rain
It's teemin' it dahn, silin it dahn
It's comin' dahn like stair-rods
It's clashy blustery rain (North Riding)
It's a thunnerpash sudden heavy shower (North Riding)

Other weather expressions include:

It's nitherin' – bitterly cold

It's tewtlin' (NR) – just a few
snow-flakes

It's white over – with a coating
of snow

It's stowerin' (NR) – blizzard
conditions

A make-shift piece of work, suggestive of something held together with bits of string, could be described as a *band-end job*.

If my young brother and I had not made a good job of something when helping our Dad, he would say:

'Nay. Tha's same as a man made o' band!'

In parts of the West Riding dialect speakers used to add an extra vowel to the 'o' sound – as in words like *go-ah, so-ah, Joo-ah (Joe)* etc.

A school inspector once went to a class of young children in an RE lesson in one of the towns in the Heavy Woollen District.

'I've a sweet here,' he said. 'For the child who can tell me the name of the man who built the ark… Now, boy! Do *you* know?'

The little lad said: *'No-ah!'* – and got the sweet.

Common farming terms:

flaycrow – scarecrow

laithe – barn

lye – scythe

mistal, shippon, coo-oose, byre – cow-shed

groop – drain in a cowshed

pooak – sack

pleeaf, ploo – plough

staggarth – stack yard

stee – ladder

strickle – sharpening tool

flaycrow

There's nothing new about farmers grumbling about the weather threatening their harvest, as we see in the first verse of a North Riding song from Victorian times:

Rainin' ageean, Ah deea declare;
It's twaa days wet for yah day fair;
Warse tahmes ner theease was nivver seen:
Us farmers 'll be beggared clean!

Talkin' o' brass (old-style):

sovrin – pound

quid, pund, pahnd, poond – pound

'awf a crahn / croon – two shillings and sixpence

florin – two shillings

bob – shilling (twelve old pence)

tanner – sixpence (2?p)

tuppence – two (old) pence

'awp'ny – half-penny piece

farthin' – quarter penny piece

Proverbs concerning *brass*:

Wheeare ther's muck ther's brass
'E's bowlegged wi brass!
Ther's nowt good that's cheap

Comical 'words' are sometimes written to show how Yorkshire speech, not always slow, can be quick and contracted:

'Astagorritwithi? Have you got it with you?

Lerrergerritersen Let her get it herself

Isezitintburritiz He says it isn't but it is

Odonwhileterneet Wait until tonight

Thamunsupupanshurrup You must drink up and be quiet

Nothing wrong in using a double negative in Yorkshire dialect, where the practice is standard. For example:

Ah dooan't want nowt ner mooare (WR)
I don't want anything else

'E nivver said nowt neeaways ti neean on 'em (NER) He never said anything at all to anybody

While is used in dialect in the sense
of until:

wi s'll 'appen stay while Munda
we shall perhaps stay until Monday

So Yorkshire drivers could be
forgiven for misunderstanding:
'Wait while the light is red'

As we get older our memories are less clear and we're more easily confused. In the West Riding you might hear the comment, when somebody has forgotten something or got mixed up:

Nay, lad (or lass). Tha's doitin'.

The Yorkshireman's motto
(said tongue-in-cheek, because we're
not like this really!):

'Ear all, see all, say nowt;
Eyt all, sup all, pay nowt;
An' if ivver tha does owt fer nowt –
Do it fer thissen!

'Yer mucky little tyke!' This used to be said to children who came in from play covered in dirt – a *tyke* being standard for a dog (derived from the Viking word 'tika').

Because Yorkshire men were often seen with a little mongrel dog, they were jokingly called *tykes*, a term now used for anyone born and bred in Yorkshire.

What's behind the euphemisms:

By gum! – By God!

By heck! – By hell!

What the hummer! – What the hell!

Owd Nick, t' Owd Lad – the Devil

Old country saying:

A whistlin' woman an' a crowin' 'en brings
t' Owd Lad aht of 'is den

And another:

Bedale bonnets an' Bedale faces
Finnd nowt ti beat 'em
I' onny places

Too bad if you didn't understand this
warning in North Riding dialect,
which a farmer put up at the
entrance to his field at Duck Bridge
near Danby:

> *Thoo'll knaw which is t' bull*
> *Bi t' ring in 'is snoot;*
> *Seea deean't stand 'n gawp:*
> *It's tahme ti git oot!*

How are you? Dialect speakers might answer by using the following, in descending order of health:

Champion!
Nicely
Nobbut middlin'
Nobbut varry middlin'
Just fair
Dowly
Badly
Failin'
Goin' dahn t' nick

Yorkshire folk can certainly talk, but
don't do it for the sake of talking.
Hence such sayings as:

'E chuntered a bucketful

'E talks – an' 'e says nowt!

Clogs, the standard wooden shoes of many Yorkshire working folk, appear in several sayings. For example, *Keep cloggin' on! Ah'll sooin bi cloggin' ageean. Ah s'll not pop mi clogs just yet!*

Dialect-speakers consistently drop their 'h's, except, oddly enough, in mild curses, where they seem to be kept for emphasis (eg *What the heck! Oh, hummer!*).

But you would never hear an 'h' in something like: *'Ellow, 'Arry! Me an' 'Arold 'ave just 'ad a 'appy 'oliday i' 'Astings – lovely 'addock, 'ake an' 'allibut, we 'ad.*

Intonation and emphasis can make all the difference, as in the way the following are said:

Nah, <u>then</u>? (Hello! How are you?)

<u>Nah</u>, then! (Here we are, etc)

Na <u>then</u>, lads? (Come on, all right, etc)

Na <u>then</u>! (Watch it! That's enough, etc)

A song that has carried Yorkshire dialect all round the world is '*On Ilkla Mooar Baht 'At*', which originated during a Victorian choir outing over the moors by Methodists from Halifax. A young man slipped away from the main party to do a bit of courting. When he returned, his friends started pulling his leg. Where had he wandered off to without his hat? For a romp in the heather with Mary Jane! Though just a bit of fun, the words have been preserved because they sang them to one of their best-known hymn-tunes, 'Cranbrook'.

1. *Wheeare wo' ta bahn when Ah saw thee,*
   On Ilkla Mooar baht 'at?
2. *Tha's been a-cooarting' Mary Jane*
3. *Tha's bahn ter get thi deeath o' cowd*
4. *Then wi s'll 'a' ter bury thee*
5. *Then t' wurrums 'll come ah' et thee up*
6. *Then t' ducks 'll come an et up t'wurrums*
7. *Then wi s'll come an' eyt up t'ducks*
8. *Then wi s'll all 'ave etten thee,*
9. *That's wheear wi get us ooan back!*

Reflexive verbs are common in dialect. For example:

Sit thissen dahh, lad! (WR)

Sit thissel doon, lass! (NER)

Ah think Ah'll wesh missen

Frame thissen! (Get organised!)

Dooan't thee fret thissen! (Don't worry!)

Yorkshire folk are cautious about spending their *brass*, but have no time for miserly folk. Hence the saying:

'e's double-fisted an' threpple-throated (WR)
(he'll pay for two drinks, but drink as if he'd three throats)

'e's that mean 'e'd nip a curn (currant)
i' two (NR)

'e's that mean 'e'd skin a lop (flea) *fer t' 'ide an' tallow* (NER)

When a place is in a mess you might exclaim in dialect:

What a hoile! (WR)

A bonny hubbleshoo! (NR)

An 'oose like Fondbridge Fair! (ER)

Sitha, sometimes written, *Sither*, or *Sithee*, does not mean 'I'll see you', but 'Look!' Short for the imperative 'See thou!', it is used to draw attention to something:

Sither at this!

Or to emphasise something:

''Eh! Tha can't come in 'ere, sitha!'

Burnin' Owd Bartle is an ancient custom which takes place every year at West Witton in Wensleydale on the Saturday night nearest St Bartholomew's Day (24th August).

An effigy of Bartle (supposedly a man once caught sheep-stealing) is carried shoulder-high round the village, with traditional stopping-places for drinks. Then he is placed against a wall at Grisgill End and set on fire. At each stopping-place and while he is burning the following traditional dialect rhyme is chanted…

At Pen Hill crags he tore his rags;
At Hunter's Thorn he blew his horn;
At Capplebank stee he brak his knee;
At Grisgill Beck he brak his neck;
At Waddam's End he couldn't fend;
At Grisgill End we'll mak his end:
Shout, lads, shout!

Local usage varies, but most areas would accept the difference between:

snicket – a passage between walls or hedges providing a short cut

ginnel – a narrow passage, usually between buildings and sometimes covered. It is said you can hear your footsteps echo in a ginnel.

A gibe traditionally said of a bow-legged man, between whose legs the runaway animal might escape:

'e couldn't stop a pig in a ginnel

A common West Riding phrase originated in the coal-mines, where children employed as trappers opened and shut the ventilation shafts by using a square piece of wood as a door. Miners would sometimes shout to them to stop the air-flow by putting the wood into the hole, hence the order:

Put t' wood i' t' 'oile! – now used to mean 'Shut the door!'

'Oile, literally 'hole', is often used to mean 'a place' in West Riding dialect:

bobby-'oile – police station

chip-'oile, fish-'oile – fish and chip shop

coil-'oile – coal cellar

delph-'oile – quarry

kall-'oile – place for gossip

lug-'oile – ear-hole

muck-'oile – dirty, untidy place

penny-'oile – mill gate-house

pig-'oile – sty

tuffil-'oile – garden shed

Various creatures have dialect names.
For example:

cuddy – donkey; hedge sparrow (NER)

gallowa – small horse, pony

gowk – cuckoo

moak – donkey

mowdywarp – mole

shepster – starling

spuggy – house-sparrow

steg – gander

stoggy – wood pigeon

moak

We don't mind laughing at ourselves in Yorkshire, as in the saying:

Yorksher born, an' Yorksher bred;
Strong in t' arm,
An' thick in t' 'ead.

A teacher had told her class in the Dales the parable of the shepherd who went looking for a lost sheep, leaving the ninety-nine others in the fold. Why did he look for this one sheep, she asked, when he had so many others? A little boy's hand shot up. *'Please, Miss,'* he said. *''Appen it wor t' tup.'*

If a West Riding person was taken aback by something, they might express their surprise by saying:

Ah wor fair capped!

In North and East Riding dialect areas, you might hear:

Ah wor stagnated!

A great pioneer of dialect studies was Professor Joseph Wright, better known as '*ahr Jooa*', when he started work at the age of six, looking after the donkeys in a quarry at Windhill, Shipley. He eventually taught himself to read and write, studied at colleges and universities, and ended up as Professor of Comparative Philology at Oxford. Here he published the six-volume 'English Dialect Dictionary' (1905), still a standard reference work for all English dialects.

One day Joseph Wright was proudly showing his down-to-earth Yorkshire mother round Oxford University. When they came to one magnificent college and he asked her what she thought of it, she simply said:

'Ee! But it 'ould mek a grand Co-op!'

The committee which Professor Joseph Wright had used to collect Yorkshire dialect words, meeting in Bradford, had completed their work in 1897. Instead of disbanding they decided to form the Yorkshire Dialect Society, now the oldest of its kind in the world, Professor Wright being its vice-president.

A farmer was noted for selling watered-down milk. So a local lad used to shout after him: '*Farmer Smith, tha watters thi milk, tha knaws!*'

The farmer complained to the lad's teacher, who told him he must on no account say this again. Next time the lad saw the farmer he simply called out: '*Farmer Smith… tha knaws!*'

Long before the days of WCs (water closets) Yorkshire folk had to 'go down the yard' to an outside toilet, variously described as:

privy, petty, nessy, closit, donnakin – and less polite names

'Mawk' is an Old Norse word meaning maggot. In the West Riding it has provided some vivid dialect phrases. For example:

a reight mawk (miserable, maungy person)

as fat as a mawk (nearly bursting its skin)

Ah s'll mawk i' this top coit (get too hot)

as white as a privy mawk (the contrast between the white maggot and the black surroundings)

Nah, denn, dee!

Traditional greeting in Sheffield,
when friends meet and ask each
other how they are getting on

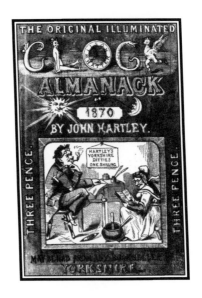

John Hartley (1839-1915) of Halifax was the most prolific of all the West Riding dialect writers. Not only did he edit the best-selling 'Clock Almanack' for most of his life, but gave regular public recitations of his own work, ranging from comic poems such as *'Ahr Mary's Bonnit'* to serious and moving commentaries on the plight of poor children in the industrial towns, such as *'Bite Bigger'* and *'A Hawporth'*.

The identity of people named in some old Yorkshire sayings has been lost, as in this one from the Barnsley area:

As idle as Ludlam's dog 'at laid its 'eead agen t' wall ter bark

Overheard in the old North Riding:

*'Thoo's getten poison i' thi sistren,' says
t' docther. 'That's why tha's belly wark.
Thoo mun 'a thi teeath oot.'
'What?,' Ah says. 'All on 'em?'
'Aye,' he says. 'Ivvery yan'…
So Ah took 'em oot, an' laid 'em on
t' table.*

Halifax is built o' wax,
Heptonstall o' stoane;
I' Halifax ther's bonny lasses;
I' Heptonstall ther's nooan.

Halifax also had a reputation for the swift execution of malefactors on its gibbet, reflected in the lines:

From Hell, Hull and Halifax
Good Lord deliver us!

Friendly jibes amongst neighbouring communities used to be common, such as the saying that in my native Wibsey *'t' ducks allus fly back'ards rooad ter keep t' muck aht o' the'r een'*.

This was also said of places like Pudsey, where they were supposed to have 'treacle mines' and where it was claimed that the Pudsey coal-miners *'all 'ad bald 'eeads – cos the' pull 'em aht o' t' pit wi' suckers'*.

Castleford lasses
May weel bi fair,
For the' wesh i' t' Calder
An' sind i' t' Aire.

(*sind* – to rinse)

Said especially of a woman who talks at length, including every single detail:

Sh' telled t' tale from t' thread ter t' needle!

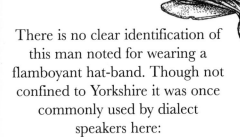

There is no clear identification of this man noted for wearing a flamboyant hat-band. Though not confined to Yorkshire it was once commonly used by dialect speakers here:

As queer as Dick's 'at-band, 'at went nine times rahnd – an' still wouldn't tee

Some common dialect comparisons:

as common as muck

as wick as a weasel

as thin as a latt

as straight as a yard o' pump watter

as bald as a blether o' lard

as deeaf as a yat-stowp

When somebody in Yorkshire has behaved stupidly you might hear them described as 'gormless'. The correct spelling is actually *gaumless*, because it means they are short of *gaum* or common sense. This is derived from the Old Norse word 'gaumr' which could also refer to paying attention or heed. So we also have the phrase:

Tak' no gaum on 'im!
(Don't take any notice of him!)

Two old Yorkshire chaps, about to pass each other in the street, hesitated, thinking that they recognised each other. Realising they were mistaken, one of them said:

Well, Ah'll bi blowed! Ah thowt it wor thee – an' tha thowt it wor me... An' by gow, it's nawther on us!

Nay, lad. Ah'm not t' owdest inhabitant.
He died years ago.

(Owd Amos, 'Dalesman')

It is said that an inattentive lad was once asked by the teacher, who had been discussing architecture, if he could name three different kinds of window.

'Aye,' said the lad. *'Oppen, shut an' brokken.'*

The verb *cap* is used in two senses in Yorkshire dialect. When somebody is really surprised they might say:

Ah wor fair capped!

There is also the adjective *cappin'* (surprising), and when something is thought to beat everything else you might hear *It caps owt!*

Some dialect creepy-crawlies:

arran or *attercop* – spider

black-clock – kind of beetle

bummlekite – bumble bee

cleg – horse-fly

dowdy cow – ladybird

lop – flea

forkn' robin, twinge, twitchbell – earwig

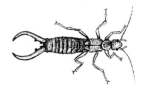

Yorkshire folk should make sure that off-comed-uns at least know how to pronounce the name of our county.

It's not 'York-shire' (to rhyme with 'fire') nor 'York-sheer' (to rhyme with 'fear') but *York-sher*.

Words from India and Romany speech have sometimes been absorbed into Yorkshire dialect. For example, in my boyhood it was common to hear *Let's 'ave a dekko!* (a look). In the Knaresborough area you can still occasionally hear *Noo then, mi owld charver!*, when friends meet – a word derived from Romany *charvo* (lad)

The traditional dialect word for 'sweets' varies according to the part of Yorkshire you are in. In the West Riding we used to say as children *Gi'e us a spice!* In the North and East Ridings, however, you were more likely to hear *Gi'e us a goody!* – as in the well-known comic tales 'Goodies' by Walter F Turner.

The Yorkshireman's Coat of Arms (a tradition going back till at least 1818):

A flea will bite 'ooivver it can –
An' sooa, mi lads, will a Yorksherman!
A fly 'll sup wi Dick, Tom or Dan –
An' sooa, bi gow, will a Yorksherman!
A magpie can talk fer a terrible span –
An' sooa an' all can a Yorksherman!
A flitch is nooa good while it's hung, yer'll agree –
An' nooa mooare is a Yorksherman,
dooan't yer see?

COP HOD AN' STICK!

A Yorkshire dialect grace:

God bless us all, an' mak us able
Ta eyt all t' stuff 'at's on this table!

Before a meal it was traditional to say not only grace but this word of encouragement, especially to children, to eat plenty of the first course – Yorkshire pudding with onion gravy.

Them 'at eyts mooast puddin' gets mooast meyt.

The idea was that those who fell for this would be so full of pudding that they would have little room for the more expensive meats.

Ever since boyhood, when we often had it impressed amongst us that we really must remember to do something, I have appreciated that plain Yorkshire command (with emphasis on the second word):

'Think _on_!'

'E's as leet-gi'en as a posser 'eead!

This vivid description of a 'lightly-given' or flirtatious man goes back to the days of wash-tubs, when the copper head of the *posser* could be seen moving quickly from one item of clothing to another.

posser

This old West Riding rhyme is about a family hiding from the rent collector:

'Ere dahn i' t' cellar-'oile,
Wheeare t' muck slahts on t' winders,
We've used all us coil up,
An' we'r reight dahn ter t' cinders –
But if t' bum-baillie comes –
'E 'll nivver finnd us!

Some of the speech of Yorkshire folk in the rural areas could be unintelligible to outsiders, as in the saying:

'As-at ivver 'ugged pooaks up a stee till thi rigg warked?

(Have you ever carried sacks up a ladder till your back ached?)

Fettle is a dialect word with various uses. Originally it was a textile term meaning 'to comb', but you can *fettle up* (tidy and clean) a fireplace or house, especially on a Friday, which used to be known as *fettlin' day*.

It can also be used to mean to get a job finished – or to sort somebody out, as in phrases like *Ah'll fettle thee!* or *That's fettled 'im!*

*Fowk are like tea. Tha can nivver judge o'
the'r quality till the' get inter 'ot watter.*

(Owd Amos, 'Dalesman')

If you happen to be left-handed you could be described by various curious terms, depending on the part of Yorkshire you were in. For example:

Cack-'anded, gallock-'anded, gawky-'anded, kaggy-'anded, golly-'anded, dawky-'anded, dolly-posh, cuddy-wifted

Who was Mrs Throp? Nobody knows, even though Professor F W Moorman claimed in 1920 he had tracked her down to the Cowling area. But Yorkshire housewives are traditionally warned against being *'as throng as Throp's wife'*, who was so proverbially busy, and who *'brewed, weshed an' baked all on t' same day, then 'enged 'ersen wi t' dish-claht'*.

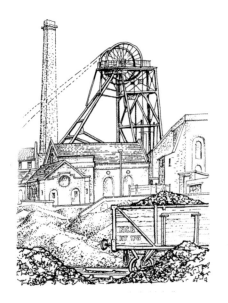

Wheeare ther's muck, ther's brass

This used to be said especially of grimy coal-fired industrial Yorkshire. But it could also be said in country parts of *muck-pluggin'* (loading manure) – and of any labourer who worked up *muck-lather* (sweat).

'Ere's tiv us – all on us – an' me an all!
May wi nivver want nowt, nooan on us –
Ner me nawther!

(West Riding toast)

'Ere's tiv us – all on us,
All on us ivver;
May neean on us want nowt,
Neean on us nivver!

(East Riding toast)

Bill Cowley, founder of the Lyke Wake Walk, used to tell the tale of a North Riding man who, when he had a glass of ale in a pub, always drank it off at *yah slowp* (at one go). On being asked why he always drank his pint so quickly, he replied: '*Aw! Ah yance 'ad yan knocked ower!*'

Two images from the old county chapels:

Een stuck aht like chapil 'at-pegs

As cheerful as a chapil-lowsin'
(referring to the happy socialising after the service is over)

In parts of Yorkshire the celebration of November the Fifth was always known as *Plot*, when it was common to gather round a street bonfire, where *parkin* (gingerbread made with oatmeal) and home-made *plot toffee* were freely distributed to young and old. The great pile of wood had previously been collected by the children who went round *chumpin'* or *proggin'*.

Guido Fawkes

Come on, lad! Tha mun frame thissen!
Tha knaws, it's Plot terneet:
Yon gurt big bonfire's roarin' up
An' rooastin' awf o' t' street…

Ther's nowt like Plot fer Yorkshire cheer –
Nay, even t' Guy's a guest!
Ah'm stalled of all t'new-fangled ways –
Ah like t'owd customs best.

(From '*Plot Neet*', Arnold Kellett)

Come in, then, doy!

As young children we would often be addressed by this friendly term *doy* – perhaps a combination of 'dear' or 'darling'. The old plural of 'children', *childer*, would occasionally be heard, as well as the more common *bairns* or *barns*, the first Old English, the latter Viking – as in modern Scandinavian languages.

Aye, lad. Ah'm ninety-nine terday. One mooare year, an' Ah s'll be a centipede.

(Owd Amos, 'Dalesman')

Boroughbridge keep oot o' t' way,
For Auldboro' toon
Ah'll ding doon!

(said by the Devil before throwing
the three Devil's Arrows)

An old chap had been seriously ill, and went to Scarborough to convalesce. He was doing well, but on the last day of his holiday he collapsed and died. At the funeral they were filing past the open coffin to pay their respects. To please the widow, a friend said to her: *'Ee, 'e looks a lovely colour. That week i' Scarborough must 'a' done 'im good.'*

An East Riding friend used to tell the tale of somebody reminding him that they were going round collecting money to build a public swimming pool.

'Aye,' he said. 'They've been roond.'

'Did thoo give 'em owt?'

'Aye,' he said. 'Ah did… A bucket o' watter.'

Roseberry Topping is a distinctive hill between Guisborough and Great Ayton. Weather-lore predicting heavy rain or a storm says: *'When Roseberry Topping wears a cap, Let Cleveland then beware a clap!'* In 1761 it was described as *'t' biggest hill i' all Yorkshire. It's aboon a mile an' a hawf high, an' ez caud ez ice at t' top – on t' yattest day i' summer, that is.'*

'Ah built it bi t' rack o' t' ee', a proud Yorkshireman might say, after building a drystone wall, for example, without using measuring tools, but only the judgement of his eye.

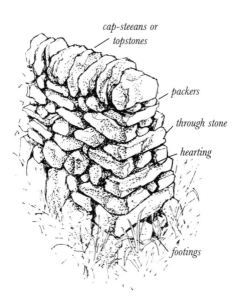

*cap-steeans or
topstones*

packers

through stone

hearting

footings

A Hoss

A hoss is t' nicest thing Ah knaw;
  It nivver answers back;
It pulls gurt loads, does a' most owt,
  If nobbut yer've got t' knack.

Ah like ter feel one muzzle up
  An' let me pat it heead.
Yer'd a'most thowt it thenked me fo'
  A little bit o' breead.

Ah offen ride on Oldroyd's mare,
Shoo's big an' strong an' brooad,
An' Ah'm reight prahd o' Bessie when
Shoo clop, clop, clops up t'rooad.

A hoss he's got more sense ner fowk
An' whippin' 'em is mean,
It's t' hoss's feelin's what they hurt
Ah've seen it i' the'r een.

(Will Clemence)

Working horses are so rare a sight on farms today that you might even need to explain one of the oldest and corniest Yorkshire jokes – perhaps from our Rhubarb Triangle:

'Mi Dad allus puts 'oss-muck on 'is rheeubub.'

'Oh, aye? Mine likes custard on 'is.'

The Tyke's traditional reputation for being a keen horse-dealer is reflected in the old saying: *Shak' a bridle ovver a Yorkshireman's grave – an' e'll gerr up an' steal t 'oss!*

The Cleveland Bay

The Lyke Wake Dirge is an ancient funeral chant sung as the corpse was carried over the North York Moors, describing a parallel journey to Judgement:

This yah neet, this yah neet,
Ivvery neet an' all,
Fire an' fleet an' cann'l leet,
An' Christ tak up thi sawl.

When thoo fra hither gans away,
Ivvery neet an' all,
Ti Whinny Moor thoo cum'st at last
An' Christ tak up thi sawl.

Fra Whinny Moor that thoo mayst pass
Ivvery neet an' all,
Ti t' Brig o' Dreead thoo'll cum at last,
An' Christ tak up thi sawl.

Bud if siller an' gawd thoo nivver ga' neean,
Ivvery neet an' all,
Thoo'll doon, doon tumm'l towards Hell
fleeams
An' Christ tak up thi sawl!

(*yah* one, *fleet* embers, *Brig o' Dreead*
Bridge of Dead, *never ga' neean* never
gave to anybody.)

A Yorkshireman arrived at the Pearly Gates. St Peter was astonished. *'Well, Ah nivver!'* he said. *'A Yorkshireman. All reight, tha can come in, lad. But think on — we'r nut makkin' Yorksher puddin' fer <u>one</u>!'*

An old lass, a lifelong member of the Co-op, had a good turn-up for her funeral. When the minister announced 'We shall now sing hymn number 528', one of her friends turned to her neighbour and said: *'Ee! What a lovely thowt. That wor 'er Co-op number!'*

T' White Rooase o' Yorksher,
By gum, it looks grand!
Sin t' day it wor plucked
Bi yon royal 'and
It's been wer awn emblem,
An' worn wi real pride –
Sin' Richard Plantag'net
Picked fust Yorksher side!

It's a champion thing
Ter feel tha belongs!
So come, Yorkshire Tykes, then,
An' moisten thi throit
Wi' a tooast ter t' Brooad Acres,
An' in thi best coit,
Or thi bonniest clooathes,
Stand up fer Yorksher,
An' don a White Rooase!

(Arnold Kellett)

An old West Riding saying warns us to be on our guard against other people with the words:

Ther's nowt so queer as fowk… Ther' all on 'em queer – bar thee an' me. An' sometimes Ah'm nut so sewer abaht thee!

As the compiler once said to the outspoken Duke of Edinburgh, on being asked to present him with one of his books on Yorkshire dialect:

Nah, think on! Tha can allus tell a Yorksherman – but not much!

Other books by Arnold Kellett
published by Dalesman:

*The Yorkshire Dictionary of Dialect,
Tradition & Folklore*

Ee By Gum, Lord!

Yorkshire Dialect Classics

The Little Book of Yorkshire Christmas

For a full list of our books, calendars,
videos, cassettes and magazines,
visit www.dalesman.co.uk